MW00723961

The
Four Pillars
of a
Mother's Heart

Dr. Sheryl Ann Burns

A Spiritual Guide to Raising Daughters

The
Four Pillars
of a
Mother's Heart

Dr. Sheryl Ann Burns

Copyright © 2007
All Rights Reserved

PUBLISHED BY:
BRENTWOOD CHRISTIAN PRESS
4000 BEALLWOOD AVENUE
COLUMBUS, GEORGIA 31904

Dedications

First, I'd like to dedicate this book to my wonderful mother, Josie Mae Pettigrew, who was the greatest most precious gift that God could have given to me. Mom, you were and still are my greatest example which has resulted in me being the woman that I am today. I'll always love you. "IN LOVING MEMORY" 1936-1990

To Mother Estella Boyd, who imparted the discipline of travailing in prayer within me.

To my seven lovely daughters who have taught me and are yet teaching me to be a mother. Josie 24, Erika 21, Amber 20, Tiffane 18, Christina 15, Sabrina 11, and Destinee 8 yrs. Old. Mommy loves you all so much! I thank God for entrusting you all into my care.

To my firstborn granddaughter who adjoins my mother in glory, my little name sake, Sheryl Katherine Johnson. Grand mommy loves you. "IN LOVING MEMORY"

Born the 9th of November 2002. To my second granddaughter, Jeniyah Manesseh Johnson, 3 yrs. old, and to my first grandson, little Jovan D Johnson, 2 years old.

To my wonderful husband who has been my constant inspiration. Dr. Gregory A. Burns, my Pastor and my best friend. You were with me through it all. The late night writings and early morning revelations. I appreciate you for always being there for me, for praying for me and helping me during the writings of this book that was given to me out of the mouth of God. I love you soooo much!

And to all of you mothers who are daily accepting God's challenge to raise your daughters according to His principles and moral standards in this society of degradation. Be strong! Don't bend! "...For the Lord thy God is with thee."

To God Be the Glory!

Preface

I was born in 1958, raised in Cleveland, Ohio amidst the depression with seven other siblings. I didn't face as many challenges in school or society as my daughters face today. My greatest challenge was being the first in line for lunch, which was crackerjacks compared to the challenges my daughters face today.

Oh I faced bullies then, but they weren't like the bullies today. There were no guns or dangerous weapons involved in my days, the only thing you had to do to win a fight was be able to run the fastest, and by the next day it was forgotten and you were friends again. There were also challenges to keep up with the latest fads and fashions from which I totally disqualified because they didn't carry the top fashions in the Goodwill.

I was raised in a poverty stricken home where, sometimes there were no meals for days at a time. My dad would feed his dogs before his eight children. Five girls shared one bed, three dresses and many tears. Whenever my mother went to church we were whipped by my father and we had better not tell it. It seemed as though our fragile little frames would have just crumbled, and most certainly would have had we not a mother whose love and prayers outweighed all the pain and lack that we endured. Every need seemed insignificant just at her very presence and touch. She loved us without condition. She never changed or compromised, God's standards were top priority despite life's challenges. In my eyes she was the greatest woman on earth.

Growing up, my father did not know the Lord, and so every ounce of reverence for God was instilled within us by our mother. When there was nothing to put in our mouths, she filled our hearts with hope and the love of God's Word. It seemed as though she had eyes in the back of her head when it came to guiding us in the right ways, and no matter what my siblings and I went through, she was always there with a hug, an answer, a solution, or a switch off of a tree that would quickly bring resolution to any problem, or adjust any attitude.

Aside from the empty cabinets, refrigerator, and tummies, there was such completeness that filled every corner of the house. My mom was that completeness that kept our little spirits high. She had a way of comforting the worse pain without saying a word. Just her presence brought comfort in the most difficult times. My mother was our shelter through our times of storm. Although many times she had to discipline us, it was done with so much love that it only drew us closer to her. Many times right after a spanking, I can say for me, that I would get as close to her as I could and go to sleep.

Many days, I can remember coming in from school and finding my mother knelt down in front of that old green chair praying and crying out to God. We would just sit quietly by, we dared not disturb her, we all knew that momma found peace in God's presence.

As I think back over my life I know that I never would have made it through my childhood years to become the woman that I am today had my mother not chose to be the sacrifice that she was then for my now.

One thing that always comes back to me, and that I will always remember about my mother, is that she never passed on her hurts to us, or the pain that I know she felt from my father's abuse. Instead she passed on her keys of wisdom and strength that she gained through those trying years. If she were alive today I know that she would say "It was

5

worth it all just to see my children loving God and walking in His ways."

I am now 48 years old with seven daughters of my own, two granddaughters and a grandson. When God challenged me to write this book I felt so incapable, I had never written a book before. But God let me know that He had given my seven daughters to me in order that I may, through the process of raising my own girls, share with other mothers the wisdom that I have gained. I don't know it all, but I will share with you all I know.

God said, "Write about what you are good at, what you are living and doing every day, raising girls." Therefore on July 4, 2000 God awakened me out of my sleep and told me to write. He gave me the title, the contents, and the deadline in which to have it completed. It was as though God handed me one of His best sellers right out of heaven and said, "Here, you take the credit for it." I felt so humbled to be entrusted by God with such a great subject.

There was a time when I thought that God had failed me. I didn't understand why He had given me all girls. Oh I prayed for a son so many times, so many years and it seemed as though God never granted me my heart's desire. I said, Lord my faith continues to fail me. God answered me with these words, "daughter your faith has nothing to do with my will, be at peace and know that I have a purpose for having given you these seven daughters. I have entrusted them into your hands to produce industrious godly, Proverbs 31 wives, teachers, counselors, etc... for me." I believe that after the fifth one I stopped crying anyway.

Bible principles teach that training should come from the home. As a result of my findings, I have written by God's wisdom this book as a training concept to aid mothers in becoming more effective in their roles as Teacher,

Counselor, Disciplinarian, and Friend. As you embark upon the journey of this book, I pray that the spirit of God will convince, correct, and convict your heart to be turned to your daughter with a greater conviction. Read it with an open mind and allow God to renew your dedication as a mother.

Introduction

It was late afternoon; I was excited about the first contraction and on my way to the hospital. After 27 hours of labor, on August 10th 1982 at 4:11 p.m., it's a girl! Shouted the doctor as she lifted up this tiny little person and laid her on my chest. The moment I looked into her eyes I knew that I had fallen in love. I knew that she was a special child and I already knew that I would name her Josie, after my mother.

After being in labor for twenty seven hours and recovery for twelve, I finally got a chance to hold her and I'd never let her go.

I looked at this tiny little innocent life, her beautiful fine black hair, tiny fingers and toes so perfectly shaped let me know that she was my miracle that God had entrusted to me to love, cover, feed and protect for the rest of her life. She had such a warm mild temperament, she hardly ever cried, if I didn't wake her to feed her many times she would sleep right through the night. Oh, if I had only known that six more were coming after her that would not be so quiet.

Two years and nine months later, on May 5, 1985, after twelve hours of labor, here comes another bouncing baby girl, Erika, 9lbs. and 1 ounce. She ate all day and cried all night. The nurses brought her in to me without me ever having to ask. She had the bubbliest personality, just a big mouth. Josie was so excited and proud to be a big sister. Just to see her trying to balance herself to hold Erika's head up was just the sweetest memory that will always remain in my heart.

Well, thirteen months later, on June 27, 1986 Amber came. My beautiful little bronzed colored baby. Amber was sickly. She was born under stress and not breathing. She had ingested a large amount of amniotic fluid into her lungs which caused her to have breathing problems after birth. Many times throughout the night God would wake me or my husband right at the time she would be struggling to breathe. Amber would have flipped from one end of her crib to the other, fighting for air. My husband or I would wake up, grab her and begin to pray as we would flip her lifeless, limp little body upside down for the mucus to run out, and for her to catch her breath. I was so tired of the emergency rooms, crying through the night, afraid to go to sleep and wondering when her last breath might be.

One day God spoke to me as she was gasping for air and said, "You will trust me now or you never will." My mother, living at the time, laid hands on her and began to pray as I cried and trusted God for her healing. It was something, seeing my baby's eyes roll to the back of her head; lips turn purple, and body become as limp as a wet rag, and then God moved! Out of her throat leaped a large form as of a growth. It looked like the white of an egg, much larger though, with veins running through it. My husband's mother caught it in a cloth diaper as we looked in amazement. From that day forward God healed my baby. Her color came back and she began to breathe normal.

Two years later, on September 7, 1988, Tiffany came. My little granny. She looked like a little prune with eyes, nose and lips. She was beautiful in her own little fruitful way. Tiffany didn't cry a lot, she just made a lot of noise, all the time. I always wondered why, only to discover that she was a psalmist, Oh my God! She is the most anointed, awesome, prophetic psalmist. I had always wondered who would possess the gift to sing like me. Well she doesn't sing like me, she sings much better.

Many years ago at one of our church's Christmas programs, my family and I had just gotten inside of the church, we sat down at the rear of the church so that I could remove the girl's snow suits and boots. Tiffane was one and a half years old at the time. I sat her down next to me, got the big girls coats off first so that they could take their places with the children's choir, being that the program had already began. I turned to get Tiffane and she was gone up the long middle aisle, one leg in her snow pants and the other dragging behind. She was hopping to the music like a little bunny rabbit all the way up to the front. It was too late to catch her; I would have only made a bigger scene. She got to the front, reached for the microphone and started singing her ABC's. I laughed so hard that I cried. She's been singing ever since.

In the month of April 1990, on the seventh day, God called my mother home. At the age of fifty five she died of congestive heart failure. I thought my world had fallen apart. She was everything to me. My natural mother, and my spiritual mother and mentor. I felt as though I didn't want to continue, but everytime I would look at my girls, I knew I had to continue for them. I felt a push of love that motivated me and said, "They're worth it." It was about them now not me.

Well, I did keep pushing. On February 6, 1991, which was my mother's birthday, I gave birth to Christina Marie, Oh she was so beautiful. A head full of cool black hair, peachy skin, and a quiet nature. Well, she grew out of that stage quickly.

She has become the most aggravating mouth in the house. She loves to boss and give orders and make the house aware of everyone else's behavior except hers.

Life was good. I didn't want to see another girl; I was satisfied with my five and was convinced that I would never see a son as well.

Chapter One

MOTHER

A mother is not just a woman who gives birth to a child, (animals give birth also). A mother is a nurturer of life that she has given birth to. You can't be identified as a mother in the sight of God unless you are nurturing the life that has been birthed through you.

A nurturer is one who nourishes; Upbringing, one who rears, feeds, educates, trains fosters, cultivates, protects.

So the true identity of a mother is in her ability to nurture, to shape, to comfort, to watch over, to protect, to teach, to discipline, to feed.

Therefore, whenever a woman gives birth to a child and fails in any or all of these capacities, she is just a female who has had a baby, operating in her unregenerate animalistic nature. God has entrusted us to be more! We don't drop litters and keep moving!

LET THE BONDING BEGIN

If a child is left alone too long after birth has taken place and not cuddled or bonded with, the baby will soon become numb to the touch of affection, closeness becomes prohibited and the ability to receive affection blocked. The possibilities for bonding will be lost if the chambers for bonding in the brain are not filled before they close. If the baby survives the bonding stage alone it will reject being cuddled or held, and will cry at the touch.

Many of you mothers have survived this experience with your own mothers, thus resulting in a numbness when showing affection or receiving affection when it comes to your daughter/s. As a child, affection was substituted with things and stuff, so now you know how to have and give things, but fail the know how for relationship. You have sacrificed your relationship with your daughter and have learned to camouflage the pain of missed emotions with stuff! This must stop! You must not continue to pass this on. You want to love, but you're afraid to. You want to reach out to her but you don't know how. You want to talk to her, but you don' even know where to start. The devil has told you that too much time has elapsed and that nothing can close the gap so don't even try. I have come to tell you that the devil is a liar! Put him out of your life and out of your mind. He can't control your emotions any longer. Help has come. Forgive yourself and your mother so that you can move on. Stop wrestling with your mother's shadow. Reach out to your daughter now! Don't let you and your mother ruin her destiny, Close the door!

The devil is determined for history to repeat itself through you. (His-story) Meaning, someone else's story, mistake, shadow repeating itself. You are the only door that he can come through to destroy the hope for her future. Don't you be his illegal entry! He'll master your past, but he can't touch your future. It is time to walk in freedom, careful of repeated mistakes from the past. Don't allow the devil to relive your mother or your father through you.

For me, being tempted not to forgive my father was the only door the devil could have come through to hinder

14

God's destiny for my daughters. It was the portal to transfer bitterness, hatred, anger, and the abuse that I had been the victim of, on to my daughters.

That was the perfect strategy for the enemy to repeat his insidious plan; he would do it through me. Well, I could not chance that happening; I was not going to be the door.

So after the death of my mother, I went on my face before God and begged him to remove the hatred. I couldn't go on, it was killing me. I was tired of masking it and giving my hatred little pet names to minimize its reality. So I repented before the Lord for the hatred that was in my heart and began a thirty day fast. I fasted so until my clothes literally fell off of me. My husband thought that I was going to die, and I did. The old Sheryl was buried. That abused little girl who would look at her husband and see her father so many days was dead. My woman came alive.

You will never be able to rejoice over the birth of your daughter until you have really forgiven your mother. In Genesis, chapter 41 verses 51, Joseph rejoiced at the birth of his sons because He said, "God hath made me forget all my toil, (troubles) and my entire father's house. For God hath caused me to be fruitful in the land of my affliction." He was not going to pass the hurts from his father's house on to his sons.

In other words, the place where you were afflicted the most, rejected, hated, envied, cast out, imprisoned, or tempted is the same place where God wants to make you prosper. You don't have to run, Just Forgive! Forgiveness is the place of your prosperity, not a new city!

Tell God right now, I am sorry; I want to be free from the hurts of my past. I will not be what happened to me in my yester-years.

CROSS ROLES FOR CROSSROADS

We live in a time of moral decline. A time in which the very foundation which family values were built upon are decaying fast. These are times when, in a daughter's life she faces many challenges, temptations, decisions and choices. I'd like to call this time "Cross Roads." There comes a time in a mother's life when she is challenged like never before to rise and meet her daughter at these Cross Roads, to safely guide her through the many intersections that she will encounter in life; spiritually, physically, emotionally, and mentally. I'd like to call this time "Cross Roles."

There are four major relational roles that God is challenging mothers in today's society to rise and walk in that you may powerfully affect your daughter's life, and help her secure her identity by walking in the victory she also inherits through Christ.

These Roles Are:

> Teacher
> Counselor
> Disciplinarian
> Friend

Mom, there is a danger when either of these relational roles is missing in the growth stages of your daughter's life. She tends to bond with the person or people that fill the void. It must be understood that bonding is a spiritual principle that is hard to break once a soul tie has developed. So if you don't begin to effectively walk in each role in her life, Satan has a friend, a counselor, a disciplinarian or a teacher to bring into her life and fill the voids. So close the door on the devil and open up your spirit to God that He may empower you to become more of an effective mother in her life.

As I continue to accept the challenge to raise my seven daughters according to God's standards, and as I counsel mothers concerning theirs, I am seeing more and more each day that one of the major problems in torn relationships between mothers and daughters is the lack of know how. I've learned that many mothers have never experienced healthy relationships with their own mothers. The devil stopped up that vein to ensure that nothing would be passed on to the daughter, which guarantees the daughter having no knowledge to pass on to her daughter.

We don't just know how to be mothers, we must learn, be taught, seek guidance, and accept challenge.

Throughout the books of the Bible are pages upon pages of life stories woven with the cords of relationship. Future generations came into existence only through the relationships of the present generation. Whatever the condition of the past generation will be the condition of the present one, and whatever the condition of the present generation will be the condition of the future's. So whenever Satan cannot stop a generation itself from coming forth, His next goal will be to cause an overcast of disease, dysfunction etc... upon the present generation with the past generation's condition, thus crippling the next generation from it's successes before it ever gets started.

Every mother/daughter relationship is targeted by the devil because a healthy nurturing relationship strengthens the future generation against him. So when he can stop godly mothers from imparting into their daughters, he immobilizes the next generation of women against him.

Women are seed carriers, incubators. It was and still is the seed of woman that bruised and will continue to bruise the head of Satan. So if he can shut your mouth from teaching and prophesying what must be spoken into her life, he'll stop the next generation of prophetess', teachers, healers etc...that have come through your womb. Maybe you will still give birth to the seed that is within you, but you will have failed to give seed into the life that will cause her to be the next generation of victorious women in Christ.

A TIME FOR WAR

It seems as though every time I turn on the television or read a news paper all I hear about is troubled teens, rebellious teens, abusive teens, teen pregnancy etc... There is too much negativism in the media concerning the youth of today and not enough positive emphasis. Some teens feel that all you have to do to be recognized in society, is murder someone, bomb a school, join a gang and be recognized. I wish that the media would focus on teens that are successful. Teen mentors, teen entrepreneurs who are facing the many challenges and temptations that life has put before them and are dealing with it and coming through victorious. There are teens that are saying no to drugs, sex, and violence and are standing strong in their convictions. All teens are not promiscuous, murderers, thieves. We have many of our youth today that are positive influences in today's society and are making a difference. Ones that have come through some of the roughest times of their lives, and by them have discovered their identities. Maybe they did stagger a few times, and many times even fell down, but they got back up again! That's what success is all about; it's a journey not an event. Let's focus on these youth.

Mothers, it is now time to go from weeping to warring for your daughter's destiny. You have to take a stand against the enemy in his plan to destroy her. He knows that if he can get you, your focus, your devotion, he's got her. It's time to go back to God's views if you have left them. For the Word of God equips you to walk victoriously in every aspect of motherhood. The Word is the only weapon that you have left and without it both you and her lay an open target to the enemy's devices.

"Every wise woman buildeth her house..." Proverbs 14:1a. God has never required us to do anything where He has not provided the tools needed to accomplish the task. For every vision He makes provision.

God has given us the building blocks needed to successfully build our homes. (Building Blocks for relationship see page 21) Not the outer house of brick and mortar, but the inner house that is built upon trust, patience, communication, and honesty. The foundation stone is the Word of God. We as mothers have an awesome responsibility before Him. To teach, counsel, discipline, and befriend our daughters in these various capacities. This is God's command. Every time you obey the commands of God you declare war on the devil, every time you disobey you come into league with Satan for your daughter's demise. So it is not all praying. For after you have prayed there is a job that you must get up and do, a daily maintenance to keep the devil out of your lives.

Proverbs 19:27 says: "Cease, my son/daughter, to hear the instruction that causeth to err from the words of knowledge."

In other words, she must close her ears to everything that is not truth. But how will she know error unless truth has been mastered in her life through you as the mother doing daily maintenance in the Word with her.

Deuteronomy 6:7 says: "And thou shalt teach them diligently unto thy children..."

Shalt is a declared statement, it means I'm bound to, I'm obligated to, I won't be stopped.

19

The word diligent means "to make pain staking effort," meaning it is not going to be an easy task, but we must do it. It is a duty and a responsibility from the mouth of God and every command leaves you no room for choice.

Paul warns us in Colossians 2:8 with these words, "Beware lest any man spoil you through philosophy and vain deceit..." Many daughters' are being subjected to contamination by outside influence. The cap has been left off of their minds and foolishness and satanic influence has been allowed to come in and defile their thoughts. It is you as the mother who is responsible when you have failed to seal the mind with the unfailing principles of God's Word over and over again. Just as the carpenter strikes the nail over and over again before he drives it home, so must we as mothers be repetitious in doing so. Not being weary in well doing.

"...The weapons of our warfare are not carnal but mighty through God..."

We as mothers must have the Word in us before we can lead our daughters successfully. We cannot take them where we have not gone ourselves, and they cannot become what they have not seen before them.

Deuteronomy 6:6 reads, "And these words which I command thee this day, shall be in thine heart..." The first command is to the mother. Whenever you fail to obey the commandments of God, you are found in sin, for all disobedience is sin. Even delayed obedience is sin. Parents cannot get to hell more easily than by failing to obey God when it comes to teaching their children. This is your first ministry! But there is one thing for sure, you cannot teach her if you are succeeding in everything else, but failing to get the Word of God in your own hearts.

Colossians 3:16 says: "Let the Word of Christ dwell in you richly..."

Here God gives us the command and the capacity to which the command is to be filled. You are not to just have an ounce of the Word of God in your hearts, just enough for you to survive, but it is to dwell in you at such a level until you are abundantly rich in its substance. Not poverty stricken when it comes to the possessing of godly principles, but rich! Rich in the wisdom that it brings, the strength and direction that it gives, so that your daughters may benefit thereby and glean from its treasures.

There can be no other influential philosophy when it comes to God's principles. Therefore, you don't need confirmation for what God and His counsels have already spoken.

Get into your Word. It is the sword of defense against every attack of the enemy. Don't be passive, and yes, you do have time. If you've got time for the soaps and the mall, a nap and a stroll, you've got time for the Word. You really do not have a choice. The enemy and his host are upon you and he wants your daughter. Rise up; equip yourself, your mind and emotions for this battle. Do not even start your day if you fail to pray. You must go down in prayer in order to effectively go up in war against the devil and his host. God is the only one who knows the strategy of your enemy, so you must daily go to God on behalf of your daughter, He knows the plan for her, she is His design and who knows better than the designer Himself. We cannot war without a strategy. All we will ever do is shoot in the dark. That is wasted energy.

BUILDING BLOCKS FOR RELATIONSHIP

1> TRUST that God has a genuine plan tailor made for you and your daughter, unlike anything you ever experienced with your mother. Only then can you build trust

21

between your daughter and yourself. Faith in God's plan must be the foundation for your relationship.

2> HONESTY Be open and honest with her. Your past hurts and experiences are for her present growing pains. They will be the most powerful tools for your present relationship. Testify to her of how God brought you through. Tell her that you did not always see your way or do the right thing. Don't began building on a superficial foundation by withholding vital information that may be helpful for her in life. Give her courage to face life's challenges through your testimony. Don't be ashamed. And please do not make her think that momma was always perfect.

3> PATIENCE Your daughter might not come around and open up at the Time that you are ready for him too, or even at the time that you think she Should. There are many other moments to be captured instead of Worrying why she will not talk. Be patient, and just let her know that the Door is always open, along with your heart.

4> COMMUNICATION is not just talking; it is sharing from the heart. Many times I have had to set the atmosphere first for openness to Take place, it won't just happen. Sometimes I'd just pop a big bowl of Popcorn and invite my daughters to play a game with me. At the moment In the game where I felt in my spirit that the atmosphere was conducive For sharing, I'd strike up a subject that got their attention. They would begin talking and before I know it we're all sharing, and they are pouring out their hearts to me. See, Satan is the prince of the power of the air. He works in the airwaves. So there must be a strategy to overcome his maneuver. I found that my daughters wouldn't open up in an atmosphere filled with contention and frustration. I had to use the wisdom of

God and set a warm atmosphere, conditioned with prayer for the Holy Spirit to come in. An atmosphere where the devil could not stay. It would get to mushy for him and he would have to lose their minds and their tongues. They would began confessing things where I'd just have to grit my teeth and thank God for His wisdom... I have experienced the greatest most effective communication as just being a touch or a hug. Even it says a million words without ever opening your mouth.

However, the Word of God must be in your heart first. It is primary! If it never gets into your heart, it will never come up in your life, or the life of your daughter. It is time out for using ignorance as your excuse. Maybe your parents did not know, but their lack of knowledge does not have to be your failure today. Maybe it was not your fault but it is now your responsibility to do something about it. Do not leave her an inheritance of your unfinished battles of defeat. We must go farther, be better, And Pass The Mantle!

My mother had a tenth grade education. Reading was a great challenge for her, but when she would pick up her Bible to teach us, you would have never known it. The lesson that she would plan to teach would already have been practiced so that the devil could not humiliate her in her endeavor to read God's Word to her children. She could only teach us what she knew, and she did that well. She gave us the greatest foundation to build upon.

After all of her impartation, I dared not take what momma taught me then for my now. I continued to add to my content, I sat at the feet of God's men and women that had been placed in my life, I read, studied, went to conferences, but most of all I sought God for more. I had to continue to increase in knowledge and wisdom for God to bring me to the day of my daughters. There is a wealth of knowledge that connects one generation to the next. That knowledge is the Word of God. It is the only true source of wisdom that has not altered from its original content since the beginning of creation. You can trust in its validity, it can be relied upon as unchanging when all else fails. There will never be a communication gap when it comes to the Word of God.

TAKE YOUR DAUGHTER BACK

We live in a time of sacrifice. However, it is not the parent sacrificing for the children; it is the parent sacrificing the children. So many times, I can remember the tears as they ran down my mother's face because she could not afford the shoes that many of us so desperately needed. Or the five and dime store coloring books, the five-cent popsicles from the ice cream truck... She would search down between the pillows of the sofa and chairs and find change enough to buy popsicles to split with my sisters and brothers. Many times standing in line at the grocery store she would have to put back certain items because she could not afford the few things she had. Therefore, many days our dinner was oatmeal or ketchup sandwiches, sugar sandwiches and even dog biscuits. After the government started distributing the cheese and peanut butter, our stomachs were much happier.

There were many times when my mother could have compromised her standards. I am sure there were other alternatives she could have taken, but she kept her covenant with God and to her children as her God given assignment and first ministry. She could have gotten a job or hustled, but we all weathered the storm together. No, we did not have a whole lot, but she had a revelation, that life's most important treasures were not more money, neither what I could put on you for the moment, but what I can put in you for a lifetime.

Do not be a superficial mother. Do not try to fill your role with stuff, which only makes her superficial, and leaves her spiritually, emotionally, and mentally bankrupt. Instead, actively participate in her life; invest the principles of God within her. Build her for her future. There is a power that is being produced within her right now. I know you cannot see it, but you best believe that all of your deposits are gaining interest! The key is you must make deposits. You have nerve looking for a return where you have made no deposit. How can you expect so much out of her and you have imparted nothing into her. You can only reap where you have sown. Go to your bank and fill out a withdrawal slip from your savings or checking, and you have a zero balance. You will get nothing! It is the same principle. Make deposits now!

On my mother's death- bed, as she passed the mantle, she asked me to make her a promise. And that promise was that I would stay in the home and raise my children according to God's standards. There were many sacrifices that I had to make but I kept my promise.

Many mothers are achieving greater careers, higher degrees, larger bonuses, climbing the corporate ladder all at the expense of their daughters. Mothers have sacrificed the daughter(s) that God has committed to their trust as the heathen nations sacrificed their children to the god "Molech." The name means king. Children were his victims. (Leviticus 18"21; 2 Kings 16:3; 17:17, 31; I Chronicles 28:3; 33:6; Ezekiel 20:31) They put them into the fire to be burned.

What have you put as a god before the God of your first ministry? What have you built unto yourself as a memorial and your daughter(s) is the sacrifice for it? At whose expense is your career being launched? What fire has she been thrown into? What takes you from her continually where she is constantly being put on hold? Her needs and concerns are never attended to because you are always attending to someone else's. Helping someone else's dream come true, someone else's empire be erected while your own daughter is crumbling. God forbids you to become like the heathen nations. Their greatest evil was turning their hearts from their children. You should not want to be successful at the expense of your daughters.

You might say, "well I am a single mother, I have to work, I don't have a choice.

That may be all so true, I've been there too. After work there's laundry, after laundry there's homework, dinner, grocery shopping etc....So set aside, at the beginning of the week which day is going to be the day for you and your daughter (children) and let nothing interfere with that. Keep it like a doctor's appointment. Show her that your word is sure. It does not have to be a large quantity of time; it is the quality of time that you spend together that makes the difference. Plan something special when you can, even if it is just her favorite movie that you have seen a thousand times, and a pizza, Oh my God! She feels that she means the world to you at that moment and nothing can replace it. It is not the big stuff all the time; it is sometimes just those little moments that will always remain in her heart.

So, It is not too late to pull her out of the fire. The fires of rejection, abandonment, insecurity, no time etc...Do it with all the authority and power that has been delegated unto you by God. Let her know again, that you care, and again, and again, and again!

TRI-LEVEL VICTORY

In I Thessalonians 5:23b Paul says, "…..and I pray God your whole spirit and soul, and body be preserved blameless unto the coming of our Lord Jesus Christ."

In other words, there must be total balance brought back into motherhood. This is only done through the knowledge of God's Word. Each entity of you as a woman must be in order with God. One part of you being out of line can throw off your whole purpose and destiny. And when you are out of alignment, she will be also.

Every time that one of my daughters had gotten off track or out of line in the past, it could always be traced back to my lost focus, inconsistencies or me being out of alignment.

There must be total balance brought back into motherhood. This is only done through the knowledge of God's Word.

Ephesians 1:17 says: "That the God of our Lord Jesus Christ, The Father of glory, may give unto you the spirit of wisdom and revelation in the knowledge of him:

v> 18 "The eyes of your understanding being enlightened; that ye may know what is the hope of His calling, and what the riches of the glory of his inheritance in the saints,

What the eye is to the body, so is the spirit to the inner man. It is only through the eyes of the spirit that you really get to know who God is and who you are in Him. In other words, you first have to give birth to yourself before you can ever give her spiritual inheritance. You are a sum total of your spirit (thinking) soul (feelings) and body (actions). If there is a deficiency in any one of these areas of your being, it will affect her wholeness. Every role, from wife to mother, from minister to pastor, from doctor to teacher rests upon the foundation of your wholeness as a woman.

Victory does not happen over night, you must be processed there. Process is continual development involving many changes. And know this also, that there is no beauty in development. Every one of my daughters is beautiful now but they did not look like that while they were being developed in my womb. They looked like little aliens! Every one of them. But every time I saw the ultra-sound I would say, "Oh that's my baby." I knew that she was not going to look like that when she came out because she was being developed. Why is it, then, that most women want to focus on the external than internal development? Even in the natural, the first things that develop in the womb are the internal major organs, not beauty. God does not want us looking good with major heart conditions, or relationship problems He wants us whole. Your victory comes through your wholeness.

So then, you must experience the tri-level victory of God. Only then are you successful as mothers. Your whole being, mind, feelings and emotions must bear witness of this. There must be agreement within you. Holistic agreement. You cannot be victorious in a shout and a dance, but void of victory in your minds (thought life). You must allow God to purge your passions and your emotions through prayer and fasting and filter you all the way down to your faith. So that after the dance is over, by faith, you can still go home and embrace your daughter in spite of the issues or the circumstances that might be ever present in your relationship, knowing that God has a plan.

Psalm 15 begins by saying: "Lord, who shall abide in thy tabernacle, who shall dwell in thy holy hill?"

"He that walketh uprightly, and worketh righteousness, and speaketh the truth in his heart...."

Here David is asking, Lord who shall dwell with you continually? And the one answer that strikes me is "He that speaketh the truth in his heart..." Which says to me that, if my mouth is not speaking what my heart is screaming that makes me a liar in the sight of God? He did not say speaketh the truth with his mouth, because sometimes we say a lot with our mouths that we really do not mean with our hearts. He said, "speaketh the truth in his heart. Therefore, the inner man, and your words are never contrary to what your heart is really saying. We do not lie and cover up to spare feelings. If need be, just be quiet.

You must think positive thoughts toward a better relationship. Remember, you can only speak it or decree it in her because it has been established internally concerning you. "The thoughts of the righteous are right." In spite of the present threats from the devil. Every potential victory begins with the seed of a victorious thought.

Paul states in Philippians 4:8, "...Think on good things..." Do not waste time and energy dwelling on what was. Think on what is to come. The devil drains strength from you through negative thoughts. Victory will never be in your relationship until you can first believe it and see it in your mind. Because if you cannot visualize it you will not verbalize it. You will never have a victorious relationship with a defeated mind. "He who is master of his mind is master of his house"

You will never be able to master your mother/daughter relationship until you are the master of your mind (thoughts). That is the strong man that the enemy seeks to bind. It is your mind. If he has your mind, he has your life, your future and your destiny.

Whatever door is left open (mind, feelings, emotions) will be the one the devil will use to transfer himself to your daughter. All he needs is a portal (opening, entrance) to come through.

Mothers, please do not let yourself be your daughter's hindrance. Be purged thoroughly. Let your thoughts feelings, and actions be animated by the renewed mind, healed emotions, and righteous acts.

Know this, that you cannot pass the mantle (a covering, a protection, power for defense) if you are not spiritually, mentally, and emotionally healed yourself. You can only pass what you possess. You cannot pass strength if you are weak; neither can you pass on healing if you are afflicted and suffering from infirmities of your past.

Satan is aware that a sick body, a sick mind, and a diseased soul will never be able to express the glorious power of God to the next generation. So you must be healed through Tri-level victory, only then can balance come. If I am never totally set free from the bondage of my past, I may as well place the handcuffs on my daughters hands, and the ball and chain on her feet, because if God does not help and intervene she will be the sum total of me!

Say with me, I MUST PASS THE MANTLE! I'm not talking about passing on a lot of do's and don'ts, customs, rituals and traditions that have never amounted to a hill of beans, I'm talking about passing the mantle of God's Wisdom and Power through spiritual transformation . Not just an empty form of religion.

You must lead your daughter(s) to God, (a well of living water that will never run dry even long after you are gone), not just church!

You must cover her more now than ever. A covering shields, protects, A lid prohibits, shuts in. You dare not smother her, but you must protect her. Many daughters have been taken advantage of for this very reason, because they lost the protective covering of their mothers.

GET INVOLVED

There are times in your life, when, your daughter might feel that she's grown now that she's fourteen, and that she now outranks you in life. Mom, this is not the time to back off and take things personal. You must keep nurturing. See it's when moms back off that everything else moves in. Here is what is going on. Her hormones have taken over; she is walking blindfolded by them. You must not back down; she will become a contamination to herself if you leave her to herself. There are dangers, temptations, evil pitfalls that Satan has set up to trap her and over throw all that you have worked into her up to this point. You have to guide her through these most horrifying years of her life. It will not last forever; she will grow out of it. And after she comes through the emotional years, she will turn around and even thank you for not giving up on her.

My oldest daughter Josie thanks me all the time. Josie has always been a very sweet and quiet girl. She would always hold a lot in. So when she would get angry she never talked back or verbalized her anger like some of my other girls did. She would always try to follow my instruction to the tee. But yet there were times when she did not always see things my way. Why her curfew was set at a time different from her friends curfews. We went through! She would get angry with me sometimes to the point where she would not speak to me for days at a time. I never took it personal. I had to realize that she was desperately trying to find herself, her value, her worth. I knew that I had given her to God and that she was in His hands. So I would give her space to come around, and after awhile I would have to, sometimes it would be nice and sometimes not so nice. Through all of the dark tunnels we had to go through, she came out seeing the light. What I did have to be mindful of is that she was in a place in life that she had never been before, but I had. So I could not be angry at her, I had to guide her. She actually felt that she had a legitimate reason to be upset.

Would you get angry at your daughter for being lost? I do not think so, so why get angry with her when she gets lost in life. I know, you may say, "Then If she's lost she should be glad for my help when it comes. What you must understand is she does not know that she is lost; she thinks that she knows the way. All you have to do is just keep driving, when she comes out on the other side, she will thank you.

See, when you really believe that she is in the hands of God, only then can you take your hands out of the situation and deal with it by the wisdom of His Spirit. When you know that you have taught, imparted, prayed, and loved her unconditionally. Josie is now married, saved and loves the Lord with all her heart. I knew God had it under control all the time, I just had to do my part.

What you must understand is that when a teenager says, "mom give me some space," they are not saying I want you out of my life. (Sometimes it escalates to that level because we will not let go and let God do his part.) There comes a time when we must give her over to God. We must let them grow up. We cannot keep them from life, but we must guide them through it.) What she is saying is, give me time to process what you have said. And believe me it is in those times that God sends ministering angels on your behalf to speak to their hearts and convict her with the very words you have spoken. When you stand on biblical principles, God is obligated to back you up. He orders the right situations and circumstances just to perform what you have been speaking all the time. I always tell my girls, "when you won't hear

God's angel you will hear His agent" and believe me mothers, His agents come in all forms.

Jeremiah 1:12 states this,"God hastens His word to perform it." Sometimes as a mother, you can do more damage when you speak words out of your flesh instead of God's instruction. There are some things that only God can do and will do when we give Him back His design.

God will only work with what you put it, only then can He perform. So be careful not to impart any of your flesh into her spirit, she will malfunction.

LASTING IMPRESSIONS

The first impression that a girl receives in life, whether it be good or bad are the ones she will reflect the longest. That is why the enemy wants mothers out of the home during the early stages of life. He would rather that first impressions be made by everyone else other than the mother, the only one who is assigned to mold and shape her character according to God's design.

As a mother, you must even be careful of the impressions that you make and leave, that might remain as an expression in and upon your daughter's life.

See mothers, you can falter, fall into sin, get up, repent and live a victorious life from that point on. However, if there was a seed of impression left on the mind's eye and it was not cursed, it will spring forth to contaminate her future.

In the book of Exodus, Aaron led a conspiracy against God. He erected a golden calf for the people while Moses was in Mount Sinai receiving the law from God and the instructions for the tabernacle. Not only did he erect the calf, but he also built an altar unto it. Nadab and Abihu, Aaron's sons were present the whole time Aaron performed this erroneous task. Later on in the book of Leviticus, it is recorded that his boys offered a strange fire unto the Lord and were consumed by the fire of God. Where did this defiled act stem from? From the impression that was left upon their spirits. These boys saw an act that sowed a negative seed into their characters that sprang forth later in life and destroyed them.

Did Aaron correct the error of impression left upon his boys minds by apologizing and repenting to them? If so history does not record it. However, we do know that the act was committed before them. You must ensure that the sins of your past do not destroy any potential for her future. How can you be sure of this? Through prayer and repentance. That is the only thing that erases the impression and curses the seed of sin. You do not ever get to old to say I am sorry mommy was wrong. You teach by your own example of humility. Curse the words and actions that entered her ear gate and eye gate. Take away its life and command it to fall and die! Every negative affect, every action or word. Ask her to forgive you now. Oh, I have done it many times. One moment of pride is not worth a lifetime of misery. If you do not correct it, she will repeat it. Repentance keeps your relationship so pure. Now don't get me wrong, I am not talking about apologizing for every time they get their feelings hurt, I'm speaking concerning the times when you know that you have been wrong, spoken out of your flesh, or acted out of character and over stepped the boundaries of God before her.

Let us pray, Father I repent for every action, word, or deed done in and out of my flesh before my daughter(s). I pray that you would remove its sting and effect that might be a lasting impression in and upon her life, resulting in the demise of her future. Cleanse me and help me to be a perfect expression of your impression, In Jesus Name Amen!

NEVER TOO BUSY

One day my twelve year old, Christina awoke with a pimple on her face. She told me about it but I did not pay much attention. About the third week, her face was inflamed and bumpy all over. The kids at school began to make fun of her to where it began to affect her esteem. After I saw how hurt she was, it hurt the mom in me.

Tina was a pre-teen and her appearance was very important to her. Therefore, her problem became my problem. I invested in a three-step facial system and prayed for her proper skin health. In about three weeks, her face had cleared up and her skin was so beautiful. She was radiant and so was my spirit. She was excited about school and friends again. Well I felt good because she felt good, and I felt bad when she felt bad. I asked her to forgive me for being too busy for the first pimple. I promised her that from that point on what was important to her would be important to me, even when it is just a pimple.

ALWAYS A MOM

I have found out through many years of experience that you will never stop being a mom. It is a life-long commitment. The responsibility escalates. For even after your girls are married you will not stop mothering them, it will just be in a different way, at a different level.

What you must do now is guide her through the many intersections of marriage. All the counseling does not prepare her like reality does. You must teach her to love her husband just as she has foreseen you loving your own.

Chapter Two

Pillar #1
TEACHER

If you could put your finger on the pulse of today's societal problem, it would be spiritual illiteracy. Parents are giving their children no biblical training and then wondering why they are going wrong.

In the book of Deuteronomy, the sixth chapter it says that we must "teach the Commandments of God to our children when they rise up, when they lie down, and throughout the day". A teacher turns every given moment into an opportunity for a learning experience. At the breakfast table, in the tub, at the park. There is wisdom that comes with every experience, which is missed every time we fail to teach, or are too busy to do so.

Childhood is planting time and cannot begin to early. We must begin to teach them early because children are sinning early. God revealed to me one day as I was pulling the weeds from my garden, that just as I pulled the weeds to ensure the growth of my flowers, so must Christ like mothers ensure the spiritual growth of their daughters by removing the weeds that stunt their growth; keeping them from evil influences which sap their strength, through teaching, training, and correction.

We must sow early. The laws of Agriculture has even proven that the earlier you sow seeds the richer and more abundant harvest you will yield. If you would look at this spiritually, it is revealed that deficiencies and disorders later in life can always be traced back to the absence of essential elements in early training, and an unbalanced spiritual education. And so to ensure a healthy yield in our children's lives we must begin to plant the word of God as early as possible.

What is a teacher? A teacher is someone who sees each child as a unique person and encourages individual strengths and abilities that build confidence and raises esteem.

A teacher takes a solemn oath to look beyond each child's face and see into their soul.

As the teacher, you must send your daughter out dressed for battle, equipped with knowledge and understanding. (Knowledge is the power to make the right choices). She is prepared for the pressures and temptations that she would not normally have been prepared for had it not been for the weapons of wisdom that come only from a mothers guidance. Even after a mother's teaching and preparation, there are still times when she must meet challenges head on, where you as the teacher will not always be present, but the knowledge that you have equipped her with will give her the confidence to stand up against opposition, and come out victorious. Every victory gives her power for the next battle, and every victorious battle builds her esteem for future successes. Her esteem is built through her own accomplishments. When you instill the weapons of knowledge within her, you give her the greatest, most effective offensive and defensive weapon of all. And it is only when she is armed with knowledge (not the finest of clothes etc..)that she becomes a threat to the enemy. On the other hand, it is when we fail to teach, that we leave her a defenseless open target for the enemy.

There are even victories in lost battles. The lessons that she will learn from them will equip her with the wisdom to defeat the enemy the next time. She hasn't failed, she has learned a lesson in an attempt to accomplish a task that will empower her for the next encounter.

I find that many mothers in our society and churches today are sending their daughters away (outside of the home) in order for them to be spiritually, emotionally, or mentally helped.

This is ok as a matter of reinforcement, but when you want someone to do your first ministry for you because you feel that you are too weak, too inadequate, you lack the confidence, or are ignorant of the Word of God, you are in trouble!

For even after your daughter returns home you must be able to maintain at the same level or higher levels of ministry, counsel etc...that has been administered outside of the home. If you are not equipped with the tools that are needed to maintain her victory, you begin to lose your daughter. So no matter how unequipped you may feel when it comes to knowledge, one thing that you are not ignorant of is your own life experiences, test, and challenges that have qualified you to be the mentor in your daughter's life. You must be her greatest influence. Please don't back off because you feel you lack the tools within you to impact her life. Don't feel that you are effective only when you are sharing with someone else's daughter. That is the most suttle trick of the devil, and his goal is to get your daughter from under your protective covering to her own demise. She leaves home, comes back and feels as if she knows more than you as the mother, and that you're old fashioned. It is easy to understand why this happens, because mothers of our society have undermined their daughter's respect towards them by always substituting their own teachings with that of another's influence of whom she may or may not know. Now the daughter seemingly thinks that the mother is incapable of teaching and imparting into her. This is the greatest downfall of family continuity. Mothers, it is imperative that you must again be the greater influence in your daughter's life and put home back into her heart as being the place from which spiritual, moral, and mental guidance comes.

Never allow yourself to be put in a place where you ever compete for your position. It is then that you become her rival, and at that point you cannot teach her, she will only see you as her challenge and not her teacher. Many times you cannot even show the frustrations that you feel. Frustration says you are disappointed in her, which causes her to feel that she's failed you, once she feels that she's failed you, it is then that she fails herself, and there will be little or no reception from that point on. You must always present yourself as a teacher of soberness, control, and self discipline.

"She that ruleth not her own attitude is like a city brought to ruins with no walls of defense." In other words, you cannot bring strength and stability if she sees you always flying off the handle. She has no protection from your contaminate attitude. Your demeanor will assault her every time and over take her, she will be angry and not even know why. The teacher sets the tone for the atmosphere. Therefore, protect her from the onslaughts of frustrated talking by making sure that you have consecrated yourself before you attempt to impart teaching and instruction to her. Your life is her greatest teacher, she cannot become what she does not see before her.

When you have more than one daughter, just as a school teacher must learn the personality of each child, her strengths and weaknesses, her fears and potential, so must you as the teacher learn your daughters. You must study each one as they grow, careful not to make them all just one corporate group without individuality. What may be a major issue with one's personality may be so different with another's. God created them different. They must be taught differently, nurtured individually. Don't clone. Build her as God's one and only individual design. Give her the individual time, patience and attention that she needs to thrive and flourish. Believe me with seven daughters it takes time and management. Just as each one has their own personality and temperament, each one has their own personal time with me also. There is a corporate time when we all come together. Even my oldest daughter who is married still wants her individual time with me, and she gets it. She is still my big boo. I cannot put her into the same category with her sisters, with the same expectations. There is another level of teaching that must be imparted.

You will never have to worry about outside influences when there is a strong bond with the master teacher. She will never be led away into error. No one else's influence can penetrate the bond of true relationship. That is why there must be relational bonding and not just talk. Where souls bond in relationship a students heart never strays, but oh how easy it is to walk away from lecture. A teacher touches the soul of the student not just the intellect. No other teacher can have more influence in the life of your daughter than you, her mother.

Some of you mothers may say, oh I send her to church, or better yet, I take her to church, but what you must realize is that teaching is not a church thing, it is the principle thing,

If it is not taking place after you get home you're just being religious! So many of you expect the Sunday School teacher, Bible study teacher and every one else to teach your daughter what should be taught at home. You put the power of authority into someone else's hands to get the message of life across to your daughter, which only causes a greater spirit of contempt to grow within her and despise you even more as her mother. This then, only results in mothers fighting for their place instead of walking in their place. You don't have to fight for your place, your respect, or your authority, you earn that place, you qualify for that place, just take a stand and teach. Don't talk at her, speak right into her soul. Don't back down, even when she doesn't want to hear it... preach! Right at home, she's listening.

You must give answers. Don't just tell her no, tell her why. No requires zero effort, (laziness says no) but the teacher will sit her down and take her time of questioning as an opportunity for teaching. All teaching does not have to take hours. You can give her a crash course on any subject in about three minutes. Heart quality will stick with her much longer than frustrated quantity. Teaching takes time and attention, It tells her you love her and that she is worth your time without ever saying it. Remember, it is when you fail to give answers that you make her more inquisitive to go in the very direction you forbid. Tell her why, don't be afraid to share your pains and failures as your teaching tools. Let her know that God said so, and not just Mom.

An experience that I had with two of my daughters concerning music, was one that I'll never forget. They wanted to know why they couldn't listen to certain types of music, and why their dad and I destroyed CD's when we came across them in our home. So I did a thorough study on music, I empowered myself to empower them with the knowledge they needed. I didn't give the opportunity to anyone else to touch my daughters spirits, I wanted my daughters and I to have that learning experience together. I invested in books, and we did a study on music, how music is the stolen property of God, how music affects the spirit, channels the emotions, and how the devil uses music to legitimize murder, sex, drugs...etc.

We had classes, I ordered pizza, popped popcorn and I taught. As I taught we bonded, but most importantly I brought an understanding to my daughters; we have not had the problem with negative music again. So let this be encouragement to you, empower yourself,

Stop the devil dead in his tracks and in your daughters mind. GIVE HER ANSWERS!

Equip her with the knowledge that will be her weapon long after you're gone.

"My people are destroyed for the lack of knowledge..." Hosea 4:6

Your daughters are going into captivity (becoming ensnared) because they have no knowledge. The devil has no pity when it comes to ignorance. Ignorance is outright rebellion against the commands of God. Ignorance is the only thing that will carry her into captivity, and cause her to become entrapped and ensnared by the devil's deception. When you fail to teach her it's as though you leave her in a dark room full of serpents groping for her own way out, when all the along you have the keys. Turn the light on, empower her spirit with the light of God.

".......Ye do err, not knowing the scriptures, nor the power of God" Matthew 22:29

You give her over to the spirit of error when you fail to teach; to never know the power that comes by it.

As I stated earlier, Take your rightful stand as a mother, and teach with all the God-given authority that has been delegated to you. Don't fight for it, Walk in it! Sometimes you may even have to remind her who the mother is, and that's ok, put her in remembrance. When you don't know your authority you'll fight for it, and in the process you'll give place to the devil to use you to mar God's masterpiece, by abusing your authority, speaking out of anger, and calling her out of her God given name. Let it be made known that whatever spirit you speak to is the one that will respond. Remember, the worlds were framed by words, which are the most powerful force within the earth. If you want her to stop being mean and rebellious, stop calling it up out of her.

I had to learn this with my daughter Amber. Amber is was my sharpening tool, God placed her in my life to make me the sharpest in character as a mother. Amber is a leader, therefore God placed within her a strong will. Not only did I not understand her, she didn't understand herself. Now we both couldn't be in the dark concerning God's purpose for her life. I would become so angry with Amber and discipline her all the time because I didn't take the time out to seek and consult God concerning this design of His that He had entrusted to me to nurture and teach and understand.

I would rebuke and scold her and call her evil and rebellious, and wondered why she kept acting that way. As I did that I kept reinforcing the spirits that were trying to overcome who God called her to be, and began to come into league with the devil's plan to overthrow her character. I came into agreement with every insidious word that opposed the name of God within her. One day God spoke to me and said, "You are rebellious, you are marring my masterpiece" I told you to "Call those things that be not as though they already were, I told you that children are arrows in your hands, you choose the direction that they should go. The good that is needed to be brought up out of Amber is a process that can only be cultivated by your positive words, undefiled with your own frustrations. Work with me, consecrate yourself for service, speak to the prophetess in Amber, call forth the good when you see the bad. Oh my God! I was so convicted and ashamed. I repented for allowing the devil to use me to stifle her potential. I began to see her as God's assignment and not just my daughter. From that day forward I started prophesying and speaking into her character and attitude by calling forth the good in every situation. So when Amber would get upset I'd just say, "is that the prophet acting in like manner, come on, it can't be that bad, I'd then gently lay my hand on her shoulder or leg and she'd just give me the biggest smile. Anger can't continue because that is not what I have come into agreement with. Amber, at 19 has accepted her call into the ministry and is a powerful teacher. So don't let the devil use you to disfigure her identity. When God asks from us what He has given to us, it should be given back to Him multiplied and with interest. So make worthwhile deposits.

SEX TRAPS

Mother teach your daughter God's views on the subject of sex. Don't shy from it, don't let her find out through the media, her peers, or by a dreaded mistake. Satan loves to pervert what you fail to teach and make plain. He will always give her a distorted view. I have psalmists, teachers, counselors etc...that God has committed to my trust. I dare not fail them by failing to educate myself. You must not allow someone else to instill their values within your daughter. You are responsible for the foundation laying years. Your daughter begins to walk by what she perceives to be, or by someone else's philosophy on a subject. Whether it is right or wrong her perception becomes her reality and the system by which she operates. You must build strong. If you lay a faulty foundation it is sure to crack, and she will not be able to withstand what must be constructed within and upon her life. The pressures and challenges of life will cause her to implode(cave in) from within, and she'll be sure to fail because of inner deficiencies.

Any vessel not filled to its capacity is sure to dent or cave in when the pressure from the outside is greater than the power on the inside, but when you fill it with substance it endures outside opposition. There can be no air pockets in her spirit.(areas of void) In times past, I was inquisitive as to why a can would dent when it would fall from the grocery shelf. I found out that at sometime during the canning process, there were air pockets left unfilled, which left the can susceptible to damage and denting from outside interferences. It is only when a can is filled from top to bottom without any air pockets (crevices and corners) that it can endure a bump or even a crashing fall. It bounces back because the power on the inside is greater than the pressure from the outside. So there can be no stones left unturned when it comes to teaching, whether it seems important to you or not. Whether other mothers in your group are teaching it or not. She is your assignment not your friends. No one else will take a genuine interest in her well being the way that God has put it in your heart to do.

Always reiterate to her, her own value and self worth so that it is never undermined within her.

Mother, you must not fail in teaching the mandate that God has given to you according to Deuteronomy 6, you must not allow any other influence to take dominion over yours. Yes, there will be temptations and challenges in her life, but if you really build her spirit it will be hard for the devil to break in and bind her mind. He will constantly have to go back and come again with reinforcements. And while he's away there's a strategy and a maintenance that you will continue to reinforce and build upon so that he has no entrance.

The problem is that mothers have sacrificed for material wealth, financial freedom, a climb up the corporate ladder, all at the expense of their daughters.

When sexual temptations knock at the door of your daughter's passions these are tell tell signs that mothers should detect (ie...irritation, boredom, mood swings etc...)

These are warning signs, you know more time is needed to be spent developing her for this next stage of her life.

Studies find that daughters do listen to their mothers, and that closeness is linked to virginity. Through much research I have found that half the mothers of sexually active daughters didn't even realize their daughters were having sex. This gap of knowledge goes both ways. Most mothers strongly disapprove of their daughters having sex, but a large number of daughters don't even realize how their mothers feel because they don't talk to them about it. The key for mothers is not just talking only, but also being deeply involved in their daughter's lives. The message mother, is you matter. You play the most significant role during this stage in her life.

When higher levels of teaching and attention are needed for new stages of development and they are not met, there is a void in her that hungers to be filled and will seek out a means of appeasement. These sexual desires are natural passions hungering for higher levels of knowledge that birth the wisdom to combat sex traps. For every action that is taking place in her, there must be an equal opposite reaction. Wisdom and knowledge are the tools needed for overcoming sexual temptations, not birth control. Educate her!

You don't fight sex traps with your mouth, hormones don't respond to that. When God wants a response from you He plants a principle, It produces a power. ".......he hastens His Word to perform it" not yours! These power principles must be put into action. Teach her:

*To Respect herself: by respecting her body and
    demanding respect of others.

*Self esteem: setting goals, accomplishing achieve-
    ments, and meeting challenges.

*Health: safe sex is no sex; beware of sexually trans-
    mitted diseases.

*Future: everything that she does now has consequences.

*Consequences of the sins of whoredom:

    >Shortens Life Span

    >Leads others to hell

    >Destroys men utterly

    >Leads to permanent ruin

Christian mothers in today's society are losing their daughters because they give too many choices when it comes to God's house, as to whether or not they are going, and doing godly things. Every command leaves no room for choice.

Until a concrete reverence for God has been laid as her foundation for choice, she cannot make a conscience God decision on her own. You, mother, must make choices until she can choose correctly. You are the steward of her life. Why let her take a journey, a chance concerning her destiny when God has given you the map for the way that she should go. What is occupying her time while you're being blessed in service? (tv, music, peers)Do you even know what spirit is entertaining her while you're at church gettin your praise on. You don't even qualify for God's new dimensions in your life if you're not willing to take her with you; In Genesis 18:18 God declared that "Abraham shall surely become a great and mighty nation..." But this was not spoken based upon Abraham walking in the commandments of God alone, It was contingent upon Him teaching and commanding his children and his household after him.

God wants your generations to come. He is an eternal God and He wants a continuous and eternal covenant throughout your seed. He wasn't just looking at one generation when He looked at Abraham, but thousands! How was it to continue? Through God's covenant written in the hearts of obedient mothers and fathers who will command their children and household after them.

Therefore, the generational blessings of the Lord are contingent upon you, and your seed being commanded to walk after you. So mom, why aren't you as blessed as you want to be? Could it be because you have a set of moral codes for you and different ones for your daughter? Is your home separated into two realms of moral codes for worship...The same worship experience that blesses you blesses her too. Are you walking into His presence while your daughter is dying in her passions that have become so insignificant to you because you ain't got time to come down out of the spirit to listen. Shame on you! You forfeit what God has spoken concerning you because you have forgotten her. She must become an extension of you for God to continue through. She is the continuation of His channel! My daughters are by my side in worship, I don't go in until I've led them in.

I remember my mother worshiped with all eight of us on the pew, and we dared not move because she had us disciplined to wait and not play until she came out. We were babies, but our worship to the Lord then was obedience or consequence.

Mothers, we have an obligation to teach her to get involved in the service of the Lord. Don't look at it as just church. It's more than just church or religion. It is the method (schoolmaster) that connects her to God. I teach my daughters about worship, the tabernacle, the veil, and they see me in His presence. Have you noticed, she always wants to follow where you go, (the mall, movies, behind the veil) Let her follow. Know this, she will never hunger for a behind the veil experience if we never get them into the Holy Place, Honoring the service of the Lord.

You have no outside ministry involvement until ministry is done at home, wherein the completion of character is evident in her. If we're teaching an endless revival like Moses said, "when they lie down, rise up..." We will have a full time job. Finish one job before we move on to the next one. That is one of the main strategies of then enemy, to cause major frustration in a mothers life, signaling, work not done.

CHARACTER FORMATION

Once initial stages of character have been molded we must trust her enough to let go. You will never know how strong she is, or how effective the teaching that you have instilled within her is until she is face to face with the test. Until she's been presented with the temptation from the devil. Rest assured that when the teacher has successfully imparted, there is bound to be a performance of an equal opposite reaction against the opposing forces. So let her test her wings, you will never know the strength of them until she's been tested out of the nest. She's got to carry her weight. Remember, the power on the inside will always be greater than the opposition from the outside. The only time she'll dent (give in) is when the pressure from the outside is greater than the content that is on the inside. Damage is done!

There must remain an open channel of communication. As the teacher, you have a responsibility before God to teach your daughter. But you must have the Word in you before you can lead your daughter. You cannot take her where you have not gone yourself. Neither can you bring her into a place where you are not. You cannot bring her into Cleveland if you are in California. You cannot bring her into excellence if you are in mediocrity.

Deuteronomy 6:6-9 reads: "And these words, which I command thee this day, shall be in thine heart;"

V.7) "And thou shalt teach them diligently unto thy children and shall talk of them when thy sittest in thy house, and when thy walkest by the way, and when thy layest down, and when thy riseth up."

V.8) "And thou shalt bind them for a sign upon thine hand, and they shall be as frontlets between thine eyes."

V.9) "And thou shalt write them upon the posts of thine house and on thy gates."

Doing what is right in the sight of your daughter is the most powerful teaching by itself. Your daughter must possess a healthy relationship with you in every capacity of your being, as her mother, teacher, counselor. disciplinarian, and friend. The teacher being the role upon which foundation is built. Even before the time that she came forth out of your womb you began to teach her, and it has been endless. The deeper the foundation, the higher the walls. So however great your expectations are for her destiny, the higher your desire is for her relationship with God, the deeper the foundation of teaching must go.

Teaching gives her the power to channel emotions and capture thoughts before they capture her. Thoughts become actions, repeated actions become habits, habits become strongholds. You cannot allow the devil to set up castles in her mind. Teaching is warfare that gives her the ability to guard her mind and heart. When we are not present to correct actions, habits are being formed every minute, that will result in demonic stronghold set up by the devil. Be present with her at all times, in spirit, through teaching, even when you are physically absent.

There are too many fickle mothers today, so fickle-minded and weak that it makes no sense. Keep in mind that these are the same type of daughters you raise. Ezekiel 16 warns us that : "...The daughter shall be like her mother..." Daughters will be, and can only be as strong as their mothers. If mothers quit falling, then daughters can stand. Mother, help her stand! I know you are saying, "I am that woman you spoke of previously who didn't have a healthy relationship with her mother, and therefore I cannot be strong for my daughter". Phooey! You can be as strong as you want to be. Educate yourself in Gods' Word, he will teach you what your mother did not, and he will also impart his wisdom by allowing your path to cross with people who He assigns to do so, in order that you may pass the mantle of strength and wisdom on to your daughter. Mother you must meet her at the crossroads of her life, before journeys begin in the wrong direction. You cannot get there too late. You must not leave her to herself, she needs you. It's hard to turn a car around and change directions on a one way street. She must not be left to her own philosophy, thoughts, or ideas, you must catch them before it's too late. As

Solomon stated "A child left to himself will bring his mother to shame." You must place your hand in hers and guide her safely through the mental, spiritual, and emotional traffic that daily clutters her mind.

I know you may feel sometimes that someone else can always be more successful in reaching your daughter than you, but this is a subtle attack of the enemy on your mind to block your teaching efforts. Satan knows that where any union is void of effective communication, there will be no solid relationship. So you must teach her. The Word of God is the only power that can deal with the will, the will determines the actions, so you don't have to force them to give up anything, just teach them to love God with all their heart, soul, mind, and strength. When affections are directed correctly they'll fall out of love with the wrong stuff, because their passion for God now overpowers it. It becomes the ruling force. Satan is walking up and down in the earth seeking whom he may devour. He's looking for openings, gaps, and voids of ignorance.

OUTSIDE INFLUENCE

For too long outsiders (teachers, friends, family, etc...) have negatively influenced and imparted into the lives of daughters, all because mothers were too lazy, too fearful, or too insecure to speak into their own daughters lives. Police officers have beaten and brutally attacked sons and daughters because they were not taught at home. They were befriended by the wrong company because moms didn't have time to listen. Therefore many daughters' spirits have been open to erroneous beliefs, incorrect sexual identities, etc... Because there has been no devotional time in the home. Mother you have more of a responsibility than just taking her to church, you must take church back home with you by daily instilling Gods principles within her. Gods standards are first priority whether she wants to hear it or not. When my daughter fails, I fail, she is an extension of me. When the doctor put each one of my daughters in my arms at birth, God was putting a small ball of clay in my hands, so fragile, but with so much potential, to mold, to shape, to build, to empower, to protect. I must be a good steward over their lives. Too many hands molding the same piece of clay will produce a monstrosity. There must be only one potter at the wheel. The upper wheel is manned by God, the lower wheel by mom (parent). The bottom wheel activates the top wheel, when you do nothing God does nothing, so get involved.

So many parents say "I don't want to get involved, or interfere, or control, I want to give them their privacy". That's the cowards way out. If more parents had of gotten involved others sons or daughters would still be alive today. You cannot be afraid to take the initiative as the mother. Why let her learn life on her own, she doesn't know where she's going. She's never been here before. You know the way, the right and wrong, the turns and detours, why risk her getting lost in the shuffle and you have direction. I know you can't take her all the way, but at least get her to the stop where God is scheduled to pick her up. You may feel that it is easier to let go than it is to fight to hold on. You may feel that it is easier to leave her alone than it is to lay down some standards and risk her being angry, big deal, be strong it won't last long. Satan knows that a daughter left to herself (no guidance or direction) will bring shame to her mother. Yes, you must interfere to get involved.

In some cases the daughter may feel she's grown and knows everything there is to know about life. But see, feelings blind perception and cloud reality. So between the ages of fourteen and nineteen you just about have to be their seeing eye. During this time they are totally vision impaired when it comes to reality. Emotions rule! But mom you have to understand that, and no matter how much they pull and tug, don't let go. They need you more then, than ever before. You'll see that after they've matured and come out of life at the other end of nineteen, they'll appreciate mom, they just didn't know. So don't back off, when moms back off, everything else moves in. She's walking blindfolded by her emotions. There are dangers, pitfalls, temptations, evil communications, etc... that the devil has set up. You must guide her through the crossroads. Yes, they do grow up.

Chapter Three

Pillar #2
COUNSELOR

"Where no counsel is, the people fall, but in the multitude of counselors there is safety." Proverbs 11:14

When you share in the relational role as her counselor, you create a safe haven, an environment of security for her constant protection. If she cannot be counseled, she cannot be helped.

A child without counsel is like a house without a roof, exposed to every wind of doctrine.

The Proverbs of Solomon, Chapter 4 verses 1-7 says: *"Hear ye children the instruction of a father, and attend to know understanding. V.2 For I give you good doctrine (counsel), forsake ye not my law. V.3 For I was my father's son, tender and only beloved in the sight of my mother.*

V.4 He taught me also and said unto me, Let thine heart retain my words: keep my commandments, and live. V.5 Get wisdom, get understanding: forget it not; neither decline from the words of my mouth. V.6 Forsake her not, and she shall preserve thee: love her, and she shall keep thee. V.7 Wisdom is the principle thing; therefore get wisdom: and with all thy getting get understanding."

You have an obligation to counsel your daughter in love as Ephesians 4:15 says, and the wisdom that she gains through counsel is what protects and preserves her throughout life.

Therefore, you dare not counsel without wisdom; God's wisdom. In The gospel of James, the fourth chapter and the fourteenth verse, James gives us the nine characteristics of human wisdom. He states first that it is bitter and full of envy. It always compares another persons actions or conduct by his/her own expectations, or ability, and not by divine wisdom.

V.15 " This wisdom descendeth not from above, but is earthly, sensual, devilish."

V.17 " But the wisdom that is from above is first pure (without mixture of your own expectations), then peaceable, gentle, and easy to be entreated, full of mercy and good fruits, without partiality, and without hypocrisy."

V. 18 " And the fruit of righteousness is sown in peace of them that make peace."

Remember, she is God's daughter, so you will only have the wisdom to counsel her effectively by the power of the Holy Spirit, you dare not take on this challenge alone.

Therefore, if you lack wisdom, ask of God who will give unto you liberally and will not withhold from you the supernatural degree that is needed to effectively counsel your daughter and lead her into her divine destiny.

When you rely on your knowledge alone, you give place to the enemy to surface through the spirit of pride, and cause you to feel that you have a right as her mother to demand from her by your earthly wisdom instead of God's divine wisdom. The devil has knowledge but not wisdom. Knowledge is a by-product of the fall. Knowledge is learned, but wisdom is earned. Therefore the latter must be pursued, you must go after it.

Your wisdom is the result of your pain and experience. Your experience is your power! Knowledge is just information. Paul prays in Ephesians chapter 1 verse 17 that the Lord would give unto his brethren *"the spirit of wisdom and revelation in the knowledge of Him."*

Therefore, wisdom (experience) and revelation (disclosure) comes by way of the knowledge of God. Knowledge is the beginning. Wisdom is knowledge tested and proven.

You can only win with what has been proven, what you have experienced. You had to go through everything you have come through to get the keys of wisdom for this present time. You made it through, you have the wisdom, however, if need be, let God purge out the bitter feelings, (the residue of past experiences that affected you in a negative way) so that when you counsel your daughter, she is not tainted by your spirit filled words.

What is the role of a Counselor?

A counselor is one who possesses the God-given skill and ability too contribute to the welfare of others. Someone who's delight is in helping, understanding, and dealing with complex issues and people.

They are gifted people who focus on human potential rather than human deficiencies.

The counselor shuts down emotional responses, gestures, and external expressions that might prohibit openness from the one with whom he/she counsels. It is all about the counselee.

It's not about whether or not you are hurt, you don't matter now, she does. Therefore she does not need to hear about how hurt you are, or were, only sending her into a deeper state of despair, depression, or guilt. During times of counsel, it is not time for you to capitalize off of her mistakes or her disobedience. Win her, restore her, again, and again, and again!

I remember the time when my 21 year old daughter thought that she was pregnant. And, well you know what it takes to get pregnant. I felt like, how could you, after all of the counsel sessions, times of prayer and travail, and times of devotion. After all of that, for some reason, she still sought for her identity in a man. She was so afraid to tell me, so my eldest of the seven broke the news to me. I didn't know what to say, I didn't know what to do. At first I thought that I had failed as a mother, then I wanted to explode, there was another part of me that wanted to beat the living daylights out of her. It was at that time that I talked with my husband and prayed to the Lord for direction. Oh I needed direction! The devil said, "how are you going to counsel others daughters about sex before marriage now? How are you going to counsel mothers from this point on, look at your own daughter, Who is going to listen to you now." I felt like crawling under a rock. "Not my daughter," I said, this is not suppose to happen to me. I took it personal, as though she had committed a sin against me instead of God. It would have been hard for me to minister had God not corrected my outlook on the situation. The question that the Lord asked me was, "How are you going to deal with it?" Will you see her as your daughter or mine. Will you restore her as your daughter or mine? He said, You will now allow others to witness what you have taught them through the restoration process of your own daughter. Live what you have taught. Restore her!

From that point, I had to allow the Holy Spirit to shut down my emotional responses, gestures, and external expressions that might have prohibited openness on both ends. Not just from talking, but from everything that would have prohibited her from opening to receive counsel. I was on a mission, God's mission, not mine.

I sat down with her, and positioned myself to listen. I only addressed the present situation without ever bringing up her past failures. In spite of my hurt, In spite of my repeated warnings and her failing to heed my instructions, I healed her. Oh, how complex this situation was for me, but I took myself out of it and allowed God to stand up in me and be the counselor to my daughter. By yielding to His Spirit, God gave me insight on a door of vulnerability that had been opened years ago that needed to be closed. This door was opened by her being violated at the home of my husband's cousin when she was six years old. She had wrestled with it, and did not know how to close it, but I did. Had I crushed her through my frustration, she would have never opened up and been healed. We would have never gotten to the root.

One thing that I have learned by walking in the role of the counselor is that mothers must learn how to listen without allowing the disappointment of the mom and the frustration of the disciplinarian to surface and affect the progress gained through counsel. Either of these roles surfacing out of season will result in her shutting down and running to someone who will just listen without condemnation, or being critical in judgment.

Why the Role of the Counselor is so Necessary

The role of the counselor is so necessary in a mother/daughter relationship, for complex issues and difficult situations that exceed the normal guidance and instruction that a mother gives.

Always remember, if she can come to you as her counselor, you have won the war.

SIBLING RIVALRY

There will be many times in her life, when she needs to confide in the counselor without the other siblings or family members knowing what has taken place. You know how everyone in the house wants to know what the other has done? Well you can start sibling rivalry by sharing confidential information with one about the other's problem, that will burn amongst your children long after you are gone. Protect her from sibling rivalry by keeping her confession confidential. A counselor takes an oath to protect. The family does not need to know what happened. "A wise man concealeth the matter.." Cover her. Don't let sibling rivalry brew, because you could not handle what only the spirit of the counselor could. Let her know that she can trust you. I don't care how disappointed you are, Tell God (your counselor) about it, not her siblings.

Many times as the mother, you will have to just grit your teeth, listen, and then speak unbiased as you would with a young lady with whom you are not familiar. You must advise without prejudice, narrow mindedness, or anger. You must speak only as God leads you. There will be times when you won't even know what to say. At that point, ask your daughter to give you some time before you answer and handle the situation in your flesh, then pray and seek the counsel of God, so that this open door for bonding is not lost. If she can come to the counselor in you, she will come again. So please, do not pay a counselor first, before you pay to educate yourself, and then use it as your own leverage to bond with your daughter. You impart! You be the iron that sharpens her character.

See, you lose the authority of influence in your daughter's life when you send her out to someone else for counsel before you establish a counsel base at home. She has no plumb line to measure truth or error. She gains more confidence and trust, and builds a stronger relationship with a stranger than with her own mother.

The counselor seeking to turn the trust back to mom is irrelevant to the fact that, an emotional bond takes place in the heart of a girl with the person that heals or rescues her. They become her hero. Therefore, do not miss every opportunity that comes to be her hero. Pass your mantle through counseling.

BRIDGING THE GAP

Bridge- A structure spanning and providing passage over an obstacle.

Gap- an opening, a breach; a space between objects or points; An interruption of continuity; A wide difference.

Breach- An opening, tear, or rupture. A violation or infraction as of a law or obligation. A disruption of friendly relations.

Definitions from: "The American Heritage Dictionary" Third Edition

Complex issues and difficult situations will come. They are obstacles meant to bring interruption, to hinder and violate your communication. They ultimately cause tears and ruptures in relationship. They create a gap (wide difference) that is intended to keep her fearful in approaching you, and you too frustrated to approach her. Maybe because of the degree of the problem, or situation, maybe it's because you've counseled her before in the same area. It does not matter. One major characteristic of the counselor is his/her willingness to provide a passage over an obstacle. The urgency is, just get her out of danger, you will have plenty of time to fuss later. That is where you come in, you become the bridge, willing to lay down your anger, judgements, disappointment, and maybe even shame to allow her to pass safely across. You become her passage to the other side. Lay down your right to show disappointment as a mother, to scold as a disciplinarian, and focus on her potential rather than her deficiencies and mistakes. Sometimes it might even be outright rebellion, but remember it is in a multitude of counsel where they come into safety. (Multitude, meaning a very large quantity.) Her ability to get from one point to the next in life is solely dependent upon you.

God will create a council, A deliberate assembly of persons gathered for the purpose of consultation, administration, or advisory capacity; administering matters of doctrine and discipline. There will be many assigned to advise, protect, and offer guidance but remember, you are the master counselor. The council should affirm and reinforce what you have already established. This will take place throughout her life, at school, work, church, and so on. Men and women of faith Positioned for her purpose.

ROOTS AND WINGS

There are only two lasting bequests we can give our daughters, one is roots and the other wings. Roots ground her, and give her a heritage, and wings give her flight, the ability to soar. You must ground her. It is what lies beneath the surface that is most important. Her character, not her personality, foundation on which she stands, her belief system.

You cannot give her roots (ground her) if you are not rooted and grounded yourself. You cannot bring her into a place where you are not. You cannot effectively minister her to her destiny if you have not been freed from your past.

You will not be able to give her any roots to grow. You will keep coming up (old roots), your past issues will continue to surface, and instead of you being able to hear and heal your daughter your cries will outcry hers. You will still long for the counsel and comfort that you never received from your mother, and the lack of it will prohibit you from comforting her. Either you won't know how, or you will reject the opportunity and abhor the thought of embracing her because your mother did not embrace you in your times of trouble. It's almost as if trying to give something that you don't even have in your possession to give. See, you can't give her anything that is not rooted in you. Oh, but you can if you are rooted in him. It's not through your mother's genes or lineage now, you have been regenerated, (regened), and your ability, and resources are now through the Father God, and "you can do all things through Christ which strengthens you." So you, Mother, as her counselor, be made whole. God is your comfort, your healer. Yes, there are limited possibilities through who your mother was, but unlimited possibilities through who your father is! Cry out to him, tell him how you've missed the comfort of your mother from a child up. Ask him to close the wound and comfort your heart.

Roots are the extension and life source of everything. A plant, tree, flowers, and family. You can always trace it to its roots (origin), just as you can always trace an action, behavior, or a character trait back to its origin or beginning.

Roots are what lie beneath. Roots grow downward and are the invisible life force of the visible fruit above the surface. As the health, strength, and beauty, of the plant above the surface is a direct reflection of the health of the roots beneath the surface, so the character, integrity, strength, and respect, of your daughter is the direct evidence of the quality time and care that has been established beneath it all. Her fruit is the result of her roots, and just as she is the fruit of your roots, so her children shall be the fruit of her roots, and it will be a cycle that continues.

There is no life without roots. A plant that has no roots will not last long. It is a seed that grows on top of the soil, open and exposed to any and everything. Vulnerable to birds, beasts, rain, etc... It has no stability, it is easily swept away from the surface. Just how far do you really expect her to grow without roots. Without them she does not even know why she is in existence (her origin; reason for being). Her roots are her heritage. They are what gives her the leverage to fly. Just as gravity is the law that holds the plane down, so thrust is the law that causes the plane to go up. It does so by pushing against the law of gravity, using it as its leverage to fly. She'll never go up without gravity. She needs something to push against in order to catapult her into her destiny. The roots that you pass onto her will stabilize her to do just that. They will ground her to strong convictions, strengthen her to never be moved from standards, and give her the boldness to never bow to immorality.

WINGS

As an arrow in the hands of a marksman so are our daughters in ours. You give her flight, the ability to soar. You give her direction, you aim her, through counsel, towards the targeted destiny that God has shown you she should go in. In this process she might get off course, but you must constantly steer her in the right direction. Isaac Newton's law of gravity states, that, "the velocity of an object does not change unless it is impressed upon by an external force." You are the external force, always in place to impress the counsel of God for her safety, not to hurt or judge, but to keep her on course, and to even change direction if need be. You give her speed, the ability to travel at the same degree of urgency she feels from your spirit, and even surpassing it.

Your daughter can only soar as high as her roots are deep. However far in life and ministry you have envisioned her going, is only determined by how early and how deep you plant her roots.

It is time to dig deep into the soil of her heart now, so that later on, when it is time for her to soar on her own she is ready and confident.

I remember times in my life, when my mother would awaken me in the middle of the night, call me out into the hallway and begin to prophesy to me. When ever God would wake her is when she would wake me to share the word that God had given her. She would always say, it could not wait until morning because I probably would have forgotten it by then. She would pray with me and encourage me, in doing so, she was preparing me to take flight when the opportunity of the Lord came. She would always tell me that, one day she is going to be taken away, (Oh I did not want to receive that, I thought mom was going to live forever) and that she was then, at that time holding my hand, but the time would come when I would have to hold her wisdom, and by it, soar into my destiny. Well, just as she said, God called her home, and had it not been for my roots, I would have withered and died. See, she gave me roots of the spirit, so even after she had been taken away, my continued life was in the roots. I was still effective by the power of the source that she had rooted and grounded me in.

Jesus told his disciples, "I will not be with you always, but I will send you another comforter who will abide with you forever." He was telling his disciples that they would continue even after he was gone. Because he, the spirit was their root and source of life. See, If life begins and ends with you, you have failed. She must be an extension of you. You must birth that which will outlive you. Therefore, what you put in her is so much more greater than what you could ever put on her.

Prepare for Flight

As the mother eagle prepares the nest for her babies in their beginning stages of life, her sole motive and desire is that one day her babies will fly. She carefully lays the bedding in the bottom of the nest with briers and thorns for future purposes. Everything that is needed for their development is in the nest. She is prepared ahead of time for what she must accomplish in them. She is not running out of the nest for last minute equipment for anything other than food.

After the base of the nest is prepared, she lays a softer more comfortable bedding on top of the briers and thorns, layer by layer. As the baby eagles grow and mature, she feeds and nurtures, disciplines and trains them for future flight. She is first assuring that her babies are rooted.

The day comes when the babies must leave the nest. They have been fed, trained, and even tested from their mother's back. It is something to see, how that mother eagle carries them on her back, and one by one drops them to test their flying skills. She only allows them to fall so far, and then she soars beneath them and swoops them up before they hit the ground. This training is done day after day, from six weeks of age until flying is evident.

It is something how a mother always knows the potential of her daughter. God put it in a mother to monitor and track the growth and development of her daughter, and to know when it is her time to soar.

After the baby eagles have been nurtured, fed, and trained, the day has arrived for them to take flight. The mother knowing that some of them will not meet this challenge without help, begins too claw up the soft bedding in which they have grown so accustomed. She claws until the thorns on the bottom of the nest begin to spike through. They have now been put in a position where, challenge to leave the nest and fly on their own is inevitable. This is what she has prepared them for all along, to soar on their own. Their life is now in their own ability to soar, and seek their own food. She knows what's in them, the skill, the training, the preparation. She also knows that their habitation must be made uncomfortable if it is ever gong to be accomplished. This is not being mean and abrasive, it is demanding a performance of the roots.

She now demands from them what she knows they have been trained for all along. See there can be no compromise for godly standards. It's a high calling, and it must be fulfilled.

The mother eagle builds her nest high in the cliff of the rocks. They are trained in high altitudes. You train excellently you get excellent results. The challenge has to begin high, and it must not come down. You counsel her with high standards and expectations, not your own, but God's. She must know that it is what God expects of her, and that you are just carrying out the counsels of the God head.

Chapter Four

Pillar #3
DISCIPLINARIAN

Proverbs 29:15 reads: "The rod and reproof give wisdom: but a child left to himself bringeth his mother to shame."

Parents who fail to discipline early on in a child's life, are the creators of society's problems today. Now the police, the judge, the military must do the job of breaking the will that the parent failed to do. That is why the civil law was instituted, to establish discipline where the family failed to do so.

The best school of discipline is the home. Family structure is God's very own method of training children. It is of the greatest wisdom to discipline the first motions of the heart of the child and to check and stop them there. Just as the motion of a snow ball hurling from the top of the hill, it may be easily stopped at first, but once it is set in full motion, who can stop it. For it grows as it rolls.

DISCIPLESHIP

The root word for discipline is disciple, which means follower; one who is teachable, or disciplined one. A disciple, or shall I say, the student of discipline is restricted and restrained for a season of training to ensure the betterment of her future.

She is your disciple. You have been assigned to keep watch and ensure that she masters certain stages of development. This is what tutors do. So many mothers today have got a lot of nerve, looking for a return when they have made no deposits. Why expect so much out of her if you have imparted nothing into her. You can only reap where you have sown.

My mission in life concerning my daughters is for them to be disciplined in every area of their life for the Lord's use. I believe that there are five major areas of discipline that ought to be evident in her life before we can truly say that she is ready. (1) Attitude: She must be disciplined in her attitude, for it is what determines her altitude with God and man. My mom would always tell me that, you can be the most beautiful person in the world, but if you have an ugly attitude, that makes you ugly. She did not lead me to believe that I was so cute even when I was acting out of character. She checked me. I could not testify, or even play the tambourine in the service if I had an argument with another sister or brother at home, and did not get it right before I went to church. I had to repent. And if my behavior, or one of my sister's or brother's behavior had become a pattern, she would silence us until she saw a continued pattern of correction in our attitude. (2) Education: When she is in school, education is her salvation. It is her first line of defense and discipline. When she cannot get her lesson, she won't be involved in anything else. She does not understand right now the importance of education. This is her first foundation for God to build upon. Therefore it is your obligation to stress it. If you do not stress it's utter significance, she will not have the slightest clue of it's value until later on in life, most of the time, after it is too late. I tell my girls, when you don't support me, I don't support you. In other words, when you can not go to school and get your lesson, you will not be involved in anything else. Nothing else is of more importance to her now than her education. Mother, do not feel that you are being to harsh when you demand good grades from her. What else does she have to worry about. She has no mortgage, car note, utilities, all she has to do is focus on school. She sleeps in a warm bed, lies down on a full stomach, wears the finest of clothes, and she is going to bring bad grades in your house, It's a shame before God. Her future is at stake, and everything is weighing on her education first. (3) Association: The Bible says that "Evil communication will corrupt good manners" I believe that when we get back to God's order of choosing with whom our daughters will and will not associate with, they will be ready for the Lord's use a whole lot sooner. God forbade Israel to associate with the heathen nations. God warned Solomon about strange women of other nations, that ultimately turned his heart from God after he married them. God told Israel to not allow their sons and daughters to marry of the Hittite, the Jebusites, and all the other heathen nations. The Jews chose for their sons and daughters. Just as they chose, God has put it in godly mothers and fathers to choose. A Mother can see the spirit, the underlying motive of no good company that wants to associate with her daughter. Whether your daughter understands it or not, you must teach her the order of God for her when it comes to association. You are preserving her for the Lord's use. I think about children of royalty, like Princess Diana's boys, they are of royal descent. They do not associate with common people. As they grew up, they went to different schools, lived in different neighborhoods, played

70

in different parks, ate different food, because they were of a royal lineage. Their parents were not going to take chances on them rubbing shoulders with people of different beliefs, customs, standards, and morals. They were protected against the worse possible disease there is among children, evil association. If that much wisdom comes from the natural lineage of royalty, then what about the royal priesthood that we represent, how much more should we guard our daughters hearts with all diligence, how much more of a royal descent are we, that we should not take the same precautionary measures to ensure her growth and development without the possibility of corruption through evil communication. You cannot be too careful, "Be careful for nothing." (4) Dress: I tell my girls all the time to dress for success. Your dress (choice of clothing) tells a lot about you. You will attract what you advertise. I will say it like this, A wolf is known by his coat, a goat by his horns, sheep by his wool. Each animal attracts what he is. What is she attracting? Her outer clothing is only a reflection of her inner character, security or insecurity. Many times girls dress to reflect what is missing on the inside. If it is love and attention, she will dress in a way to attract what she feels will appease or fill the void. A young lady who is confident does not have to show what she knows, she is secure and does not need the acceptance of anyone to validate it. I Teach my girls to be temperant in all things. Whatever you wear, look like a respectable lady. (5) Prayer: Her vehicle to transport her to wherever she wants to go in Life. When you teach her to have a strong foundation in prayer, she will have a strong foundation in everything. I tell my daughters all the time, that every failure in their life is the result of a prayer failure. Somewhere you failed to pray. When she is disciplined to seek God in all her ways, He will direct her path.

BE STRONG

I believe that the greatest challenge for any mother having to operate in the role of the disciplinarian, is to never allow the roles to interfere when correction is needed . You must not be afraid to discipline. When you do so, you withhold from her the fire of God that is needed to harden the clay in all the right areas. Proverbs 19:18 says. "Chasten thy son while there is hope, and let not thy soul spare for his crying." Proverbs 23:13 says: "Withhold not correction from the child: for if thou beatest him with the rod, he shall not die." (V.14) "Thou shalt beat him with the rod, and shalt deliver his soul from hell." Now we know when the Bible says beat, it means to flog or whip, it does not mean to abuse by beating unmercifully, however you must bring order and alignment in her life. How is it that mothers can agree with the Bible up to a certain point, but when they get to this part they want to shun from it. My Bible says that, "If I offend in one point of the law, I am guilty of the whole law." This is God's order. Who told you that you can pick and choose? Because so many mothers have failed in the area of discipline, God had to raise up a civil government. The police officers have had to save many sons and daughters from hell. Military sergeants have had to step in and do the discipline that God wanted done in her life, because mothers failed. The judge has had to, even the doctor. However, we don't press charges against them, even though it is magnified many times greater. See God really does not care what agent He uses, as long as she is disciplined for the Lord's use.

The discipline of the Lord through you as the mother is never meant to crush her personality, character, or esteem.

It is to never change the energy of the will, only to give it positive shaping and direction.

I don't claim to know it all, but what I do know and have learned by experience, I will share with you. Mother, there must be consequences for unacceptable behavior! When there is not, we send the message to her that she can live life with no boundaries, that she does not have to be responsible for her own actions. Where there are no consequences, there will be no boundaries, and you lose her. She ends up in a danger zone that you could have prevented. Look beyond those tears coming from the face of your baby girl, and set some high standards with strong consequences, so that she will think twice before going in a way that was forbidden again.

Strong discipline makes for strong morals and character. Remember, we discipline because we love, because we care, not out of anger or retaliation. It is so sad to see role reversal in this day and time. Since the mothers did not whip the daughters, the daughters are whipping the mothers.

If you are one of those soft hearted mothers who just can't stand to see your daughter cry even when you know she has willfully disobeyed you, get some help. When you begin to see your acts of discipline as you defending the law of God, it will create a holy indignation within you against the spirit of disobedience and rebellion. Do not allow that spirit to be loosed in your home. Bind it up! Educate yourself through God's Word on how and when to discipline. Get under a more older and wiser woman who has mothered girls, ask her to mentor you so that your daughter is not without guidance and direction. She must never feel that you cannot handle her behavior or that you have lost control. Whenever a daughter feels that her mother has no control over her, she will be left with the feeling of a lost heritage. Discipline speaks heritage. Many

73

foreign countries that I have studied are known for their heritage and customs through their disciplines. Kuwait is one of them. My god-daughter was there for some time during the war. She told me of their strict customs that give them their heritage. They are known for their justice system, and because of it there are so fewer crimes than here in the U.S. She told me that you can't eat in public, chew gum in public, or talk loud in the streets. You will be arrested on the spot. It may seem stiff to us but it is their heritage, they know who they are. Although different, it is their identity. A girl searches endlessly, when she is left without a heritage. She feels that she has no value, and where no value has been set, the highest bidder wins. The devil is bidding for your daughter, but he can't have her if she is grounded in discipline.

TAKE CONTROL

As a child, my mother did not allow my sisters and I to stay the night over everybody's house. As a matter of fact I can't remember one house other than my grandmother's. She was very careful during the early times of character development. We were not allowed where the Spirit of God did not reign. It did not matter how much I cried to go over my friends houses, if she did not know them, I could not go there. No meant no.

You have got to allow God to toughen your spirit so you won't break down. You are the steward of her life. You must save your daughter, it is not the laws responsibility! Her salvation will come through God's direction and your discipline. Direction without discipline results in disaster. Daughters are being lost in the streets, because mothers have lost the gall to discipline in the home. Mothers have let

74

the devil come up in their home, straight from hell, and tell them that when they discipline they are abusing, and they are going to raise abusive children. You are not going to raise abusive children if you discipline. It seems to me that all the murder and abusive behavior started when discipline stopped, when prayer was taken out of the schools. Years ago, the teachers whipped our behinds right in school. As a result of it, there were less fights, and school deaths were unheard of. Children were accountable to the teachers for their behavior, they knew the consequences. But then paddling was taken out of the schools, and when discipline and prayer was taken out, Satan and his demons marched in. Prayer and discipline were the guards that stood at the gates of our schools to ensure the safety of proper principles being instituted.

If you don't whip them the cops will kill them, the drug dealer will pull them, the pimp will entice them. Give limits, set boundaries.

I pray for the parents of the sons and daughters that have been murdered because someone failed to get involved. Bombs were built right up in the parents homes, and they did not even know it, because they did not want to trespass on the child's privacy. Phooey! What privacy? What bills do they pay. Take the hinges off the door!

DISCIPLINE VS. ABUSE

A disciplinarian corrects and rebukes without ever damaging the esteem or character of the child. Whenever the image or the identity of your daughter is changed, you are abusing her. Just as the potter molds and not mars, you are the potter assigned to form character and behavior, to change behavior not identity.

Discipline must always be done based on what has been taught first. You have no foundation on which to discipline if you have not taught her how to prevent certain behaviors.

Abuse is when you discipline and she is void of teaching. Why? You have not taught her what to do, which way to go, and that whatever you are reprimanding her for is wrong. Therefore, it sets up anger, bitterness, hatred and violence instead of obedience. You tend to draw out what is not in her power to give or perform.

I have counseled mothers who only discipline when they are angry, this is abuse because it is done out of an unruly spirit, aimed toward no destined goal. It is unconstructive, not edifying for her development mentally or emotionally. All that is going into her spirit, which can only, in time bring forth the same seed of anger. You must only discipline out of love, because you love her.

God only disciplines those He loves. He does not bother everybody who is bad, and makes Him angry, only those He loves. As a mother, we don't go around messing with everybody else's children in school, or on the playground. If there is some misbehaving going on and our child is in it, she is the one that gets snatched. If we did not love her, we would not correct her. It takes love to correct. Abuse mars the good, discipline corrects the bad and praises the good.

Say that I saw my daughter walking out in front of a truck, or playing around a poisonous snake, my love for her would provoke me to snatch her out of the way of either one. How could I say that I love my daughter, see her going in the way of harm or danger and not correct her path.

God will always allow you as the mother to see potential, negative character formation for you to correct it before it is set.

BONDING THROUGH DISCIPLINE

I have experienced through raising my girls, and still am, that some of the closest times with my daughters when they were younger, was right after a good spanking, after having warned them over and over again of their unacceptable behavior. They did not run away, they cuddled me more than ever. They didn't even want to go with anyone else. You know how daddy will reach for them to comfort them after a spanking, oh no, they just wanted me. I wondered, what was that all about. It was about love, even though their feelings were hurt, more so than anything else, they still embraced me, because they knew it was for their good. Just as we do when God gives us a good scolding, we love Him even more for His care and concern enough to correct us.

I remember some years ago, my daughter Amber said to her friend at church, "go ahead tell my momma, she ain't gonna do nothing, she always says that she is going to whip me and she never does" This statement was made after I had warned her that I was going to spank her because her friend had told me of behavior that Amber and I had talked about, and she had been corrected of many times, and told not to let it happen again. I felt as small as an ant. I felt like a liar to my daughter, and I had lied. Well I fixed that, and I never heard that come out of anyone of my girls mouths again.

My threats of punishment only resulted into worse behavior, because I set no boundary for her to respect and fear crossing. Since there were no consequences, she went even further. See, you get a ticket when you run a red light. Oh, you might get a warning the first time, and then you might not, based on the severity of the offense.

Let's look at curfews. If a curfew is set at 10:00 p.m. then the choice is 10:00 p.m. and not a minute after, or she can stay in the house. My oldest daughter attended high school with a beautiful girl friend of hers. Her mother gave her no limits, and set no boundaries. She came and went as she chose to. Well one night, out joyriding with friends after 11:00 p.m., she died in a horrible car crash at the tender young age of fourteen. My daughter would always wonder why she was never allowed to be out after her curfew. I don't believe that I ever had to have that discussion again. If this child's mother had of given her choices, and set limits, I believe that her daughter would still be alive today. You can't worry about her being angry with you, she'll get over it. I would rather her be angry, than dead, without another opportunity to get it right with God.

This time of discipline in her life is not the time to be her friend. You are responsible for setting character for the rest of her life. If you do not discipline now, she will not know boundaries even after she is grown up. She will be a headache and a problem to her husband, her pastor, her boss, and will become very unproductive in life. Your obligation is to teach her responsibility.

If you divide that word in two, you get response/ability, or the ability to respond in life to any and everything that comes her way. To remain rooted and grounded through discipline. Her will already be broken so that she is of the ultimate use for God. This is your job as her mother. She does not have to be sent off to boot camp for her will to be broken, start a boot camp right up in your home, you and God can get the job done.

I can remember so many times as a child, when I new that I had done wrong, and I had it coming. I would try to get over on my mother. I wanted the mommy role to sympathize with my tears, but she never spared for my crying. When discipline was needed she executed. If she would have crossed roles and spared for my crying, I would have always played on that weak area and gotten out of a good spanking when it was most needed to correct and mold my character and behavior.

I am a mother now, and I know that there are times when I see tears running down my baby's face before a spanking, a scolding, or a time-out when that mommy role wants to jump right out of my skin and rescue my baby, and the role of the disciplinarian has had to be firm. It is that tough love that is needed for the molding. Where there is no discipline, there will be destruction.

The spirit that you speak to is the one what will come forth. Even in disciplining, you cancel out the wrong spirit, behavior, and conduct by nurturing the correct spirit through the power of positive words. Words create and bring into existence. Therefore, you must always be careful of what you release out of your mouth concerning her. Discipline is not always physical punishment, or verbal correction. The most proven and effective form of discipline is teaching her to discipline herself.

Mother, the disciplinarian does not bail the daughter out of every situation that she creates for herself. There comes a time that she must be responsible for her own actions.

Chapter Five

Pillar #4
FRIEND

"A friend loveth at all times"

The most genuine test of love is when you give love knowing that the recipient of your love has nothing to give in return. This is how it is when you must give her the love and attention that she so desperately needs to grow and develop. It is when you feel that she has given you nothing in return, that unconditional love must still show. Love is not genuine until you are put in a place to exercise it when you have absolutely nothing to benefit in return. Give, sow the seed, and believe that you're going to reap a harvest in return. You will see her spring forth as a bud and blossom into a beautiful rose. But you must befriend her, you must let her know that you love her at all times; through the good times, bad times, and the ugly times. It won't be as though you love what she does, but never let what she does hinder your expression of love for her, that is what keeps her growing. Know this mother, that your pain runs as deep as your love, so however deep your love runs, that's just how deep the pain of disappointment and frustration will be.

However, that is just how deep the reaction of your love must be expressed.

As her friend you must be a part of her dream. You must encourage her to become and do whatever it is that she believes she can become and do. Don't pour water on the flame of her potential by letting her see doubt in you, or hear doubt from you. She will not feel that you doubt the dream in her, she will feel that you doubt her. Friends believe in one another. Friends help friends succeed. Friends support one another, even when it is not their dream. Most of all, friends can confide in one another without ever worrying about their business leaking out.

Where there is no vision, she is sure to perish. She too has a vision, it may be small to you, but it will mature. Listen to what she has to say, be interested in what she is interested in. It may not be so clear, but just help her get the clear picture. It may be a little fuzzy at first but you can help her adjust the views. Don't ever turn her off, because she will fear to ever dream again; it is where you stop expressing your love for her that she begins to wither, and If you don't let her dream she'll die.

Let her dare to have her own dream. It does not have to be like what you expected her dream would be. It might be totally, totally different from yours, but it's ok, you don't want her to be like you, when it comes to her dream, you want hers to be like her, her ideas, her perception, you just want to help guide them and give them clarity. It's ok for her to be her.

Maybe you are afraid to let her dream because you failed, mom, at an attempt, or in an endeavor to accomplish a task or capture a dream, but don't let your past failures hinder her present possibilities. You must help her through her intersections with your knowledge of the road. Don't let your past disappointments or failures set up detours for her and block her present progress, because you went down that road thirty years ago and wrecked. There has been some improvements, things have changed. She has a designated driver, you and God. She does not necessarily have to travel the same route you traveled, she has new ventures, new revelation, fresh ideas, and a fearless attitude.

If you read in the scriptures, you will find that there is a multiplied measure of anointing that should pass from one generation to the next, when a son or a daughter is walking in covenant relationship with their mother or father's impartation. Jessie walked in a 30-fold measure of prosperity and anointing. David, Jesse's son walked in a 60-fold measure, and Solomon, David's son, walked in the 100-fold measure of the anointing. Let her walk in her multiple measure, her 100 fold. Don't keep her limited to the measure that you walked in, release her. Always let her know you are there, and that you believe in her 110 percent. Don't try to live your life through her, let her be herself in every aspect of her God-given ability.

Can you be your daughters friend without marring or undermining your authority in other roles? Sure you can, you can do all things through Christ, but the key to that verse of scripture is "...through Christ that strengthens..." or anoints you to do so. You must be anointed to be her friend. You have to know when she needs a friend and when not. All you have to do is trust God. The anointing will never allow roles to cross or interfere with another. Just think of what would happen if she really trusted you as a friend. You could win her trust, share her secrets, and just how many mistakes could be avoided just by her knowing that you are anointed to walk in divine order concerning your roles and her needs.

For some of you mothers, you will never be your daughters friend until you have been successful at being her mother, her teacher, her disciplinarian, and her counselor; and then she will turn around and thank you, because of the difference you will have made in her life. Because of the accomplishments, achievements, and investments that have come to full maturity in her life, and even she can see the returns of them. One day she will be honored to befriend the qualities, morals, and standards that you stood for and desire them for her own daughter. That is the reward of mothering, you blossom a friend.